-INE

-INE

-INE

-INE

the

-INE

POEMS

& a few others by

BART ALBERTI

In the Manner of Animals

Hsin-I photographs by

SALLY LARSEN

solo
zone

SAN FRANCISCO

2000

Published in the USA by SoloZone Publishing

Box 410792, San Francisco CA 94141-0792.

Online at www.solozone.com

Book design by Charles Wehrenberg

ISBN 1-886163-07-3

FIRST EDITION

contents

-ine poems

In the Manner of Animals

Hsin-I photographs

And a Few Other Poems

dedicated

to all the

women I love

Amine

Am I in? in luck? in gear? in time?
in the game? Am I mine? What is my
identity? What nitrogen over rules
my vowel filled soul? With what amine
do I play? In the what worldly gestures,
in the contestation of the which molecules,
what concrete scraping and bending
of grainy crystals, crystalline edges
and surfaces will make me mine, or think
that I am mine? Antiquity... futurity...
are only chemistry. And what colors it?
Xanthine—after which subtlety, coffee,
or tea or aphrodisia of chocolate? You
did not know of the amorous ancient nuns
of Chiapas in the days of the conquistadors
who mixed bitter chocolate and sweet milk,
the concoction of love these last centuries,
since the one we call the Sixteenth, for those
who wear the ermine, or the black cloak
of secrecy or despair? The Family of Love
waits in old Antwerp, the prevailing winds,
the call of a parrot, the tea of Freedom...!

Aquiline

things have not yet been created
they feel the lack of a reason to be,

emblems of themselves, anecdotes
of metaphysics: there is the thing,

there is an image of the thing
looked at in a certain way.

Can't you see the thing's action
before it has begun to be,

its passion provoking you to attention,
to the attention of its intended action?

And how will you grasp the thing,
heel to toe, where it is, the eyesight

becoming a foothold in the snippy
passage from non-being to enactment?

You do not foresee the mere future
in things, you can contemplate,

as though whether it will be
or no is no question but only

a sight, a glance into eternity
whose wings flutter about your eyes.

Asinine

Furfuraceous, scruffy, good
for laughs, a stubborn problem

for beginners, a novice's
demeanor, a somebody's

nobody riding the donkey
to Jerusalem, *l'histoire*

du moyen âge, palm fronds
over big ears which are ears

to hear the proposition.
On the bridge of asses I

believe because it is absurd.
The brigade of asses is a proof

of triangles. The only truth
or argument is a haw-haw. And

the little simple truth of
devotion and faith is so, too.

I wanted to be more profound,
like the other animals, juicy,

sonorous, evocative, but I only
can just plod along the derisory

divine path that leads I'm sure
nowhere, not even to salvation.

Australopithecine

They paint reindeer and mammoth
on walls in the flickering,
flaring light of oily wicks.

Evoking a feeling
(thereby manifesting a will)
is akin to forming a shape:
at the count down to evolution
the crimson walls of the arena
faded to dark pigeon blood
space around *A. Prometheus,*
the tamer of fire.

The Champion stumbled:
Ho! Master Peter,
pour another drink!

Bovine

cf. BAAL, the bull, conqueror, the IT with balls
versus the cow and the story, *id est*, of Jeze*bel*,
sacred prostitution and child sacrifice,
or Hanni*bal*, the relentlessly Phoenician war-
lord of Carthage, sending elephants, war-elephants,
not cows or bulls or icons (icons are
Byzantine, *later, please*), across the Alps:

the holy Cow grazes placidly as the bumblebee
flits about the buckwheat and the millet,
the yoked oxen (before horses) plowing.
She looks up quizzically and emits a question:

What is the name of the enigmatic essence
of the Enigma Deity who bedevils us
with riddles? Shall we not be rid at once
of this nuisance, have quittance of the impotent
puissance? Isn't it *Beel*zebub, the shameful?

Canine

Gruff as a fireman, useful
as a philosopher, running

ideas around like bones,
dousing conflagration

with spittle and yelps and big
efforts, his spots attract

attention. His paws scratch
at the ground digging rooted

truths that feel good to eat
and are otherwise solid. Lithe

probationer of experience,
greyhound, bloodhound,

what do your watery eyes see
which your mouth expresses

in useless barking
and wagging of tail?

Caprine

or goat-like in gambols: imagine
them dancing the quadrille in high
craggy kicks from their cloven heels
in the tenth sign of the Zodiac
under a splinty, frisky winter sunlight
under a perfumed, capric, mystic, acidic
moonlight, in high aristocratic abandon,
at the heights of dance at mere pleasure
(or is it a diabolical, horripilation
Goethe imitation of a Witches' Sabbath,
or merely a whimsical he-goat, bleat,
and she-goat routine? "I didn't come
delicately to dance the minuet,"
said the revolutionary French lawyer,
covering all his bases). Jump-off
points are on offer to the suicide types
not capricious but intent, witnessed
by billy beards as sure footed goats toss
coins over cliff edges, sounding the note
of chance and fate, "metaphysical withal..."
Look! At the Spanish Riding School in Austria,
horses, too, kick out their legs, a capriole;
neigh sweetly for their well equipped trainers,
perform their ordered paces to an orchestra
which plays a capriccio under the fig tree.
Such "caper nimbly before a lady's chamber..."

Chimerine

“As dragonflies catch fire...,”
flitting swiftly over round wet wells;
as the violin plays emitting sheer notes
of dragon’s blood; as the image forms
on the plate of the hurt engraver
(embowered by heartfelt snapdragons)...,
a house is set to the dragon geomancer:

He lies under the rivers and lakes
of China, spirit of the waters,
who emerged at the Yellow River
giving the sage the secret of writing,
he, who does not hear with his ears,
but through his horns, having no ears.
A brilliant pearl suspended from his neck
represents the sun, controller of waters,
father of emperors, whose bones or saliva
heal, who has the secret of invisibility.
Wingless, they rise into air by power alone,
the celestial dragons who guard the abode
of the gods. Some are small as silk
caterpillars; all grow or slim at will,
numberless as the fish of the deep;
apparent as clouds which vanish
triumphantly at a glimpse.

Columbine

BUTTERCUP: a flower resembles
a group of pigeons, crows' foot;

a HARLEQUINADE, a riot of color
a floral comedy, many colored

footfalls echo, a stage play
whose actors are stalks and leaf:

the comedy of errors: not butter-
and-eggs, a kind of toad's flax,

two tones of yellow, or butter bean,
or butterbur, the butterine wrap up,

not, certainly, butter of antimony,
a metallic pigment or medicine,

will cure your funny bone quick,
while an infusion is remedial,

seeds of rock-bell, for fever and ache.
Yes, Columbina has fallen in love, all

fever and butter-fingers. The stage
manager, i.e. God, will sweep up

the parti-colored mayhem with branches
of butcher's broom, clusters of white

flowers with red berries.

Corvine

is this the bird that haunts the Bronx
and draws the jackdaw mimicry? as the bird flies
over the gorge of the River Bronk*, FRANCE
applies *under the moon, gibbous, birds, ominous*.

from the rooky wood, wings flutter....
about the little shack in Fordham (next
to the civilized Jesuits "drinking their port
and disdaining to talk theology"),
and the pendulum clock swings, to and fro,

the huge door, hinged, opens from which emerges
the figure, Cyclopean, one-eyed, on whose shoulder
the black clad raven emits from its beak the cry,
unequalled, unquelled, of *Nevermore*.

*William Bronk of Hudson Falls, NY, noted poet,
See obit New York *Times*, February 25, 1999.

Divine

Large notions of theology: super-
abounding superlatives, mega-, magna-
Infinity (if you add to infinity,
what do you get or get usefully,
mathematician?): AND if art is a kind
of *mathesis universalis* of the divine
anima mundi: who was then the *demiurgus*?
Why then, we can all speak impressed Latin
and write italic type. What buckets
of ink (an inked Infinite and linked
to print) we do spill as we are hoist
by our own petard as we endeavor
to step on the step ladder to heaven
which creaks under our weighted tread?
Remember, a Jacob's ladder is found
useful in maritime service.

Equine

They are turning my hooves to glue,
I, who was the neighsayer,
whose mane bestrode the high wind
at dawn under shaggy skies and dappled
maples. Whoso, the name was spoken
in whispers by touts, by the thin
hipped jockeys, by stunning girls
in jodhpurs riding my back sidesaddle,
by swaggering horsemen flashing
swords on behalf of the Emperor,
by the clip-clop drayman with bells,
by anybody needing a little height
to their eyes, muscle to their legs.
No, I am not a chimera, fabulous,
lion's head, goat's body, serpent
tail, nor a sphinx, the strangler.
Let me tell just you, I, who likes
sugar cubes. Comb my mane, nuzzle
my muzzle as I whinny the same old
stories you heard before.

Ermine

the herald shows black dots on a white field:
stout judges wear the robes of the turncoat
weasel who changes color with the season.
The stoat becomes quickly valuable in winter,
changing black to white like an autumnal lawyer,
when "pop goes the weasel" plays off a symphony
orchestra with the royal court cavorting
over hill and dale in snowshoes, shotguns
and popguns in the crook of the elbow. Mouse-
snaps too small for him; bear traps, too big;
the seasoned hunter squints in a white daze,
a figure out of Bruegel with trap and club
as laughing peasants pull out hot odorous
loaves from ovens free from servile tenures.

Feline

It shows the note of Zen:
what is the sound of one paw

clapping? of all four sitting
still as a cucumber? Fur-balls

shedding wisdom, like the cat
i' th' fable, no reciprocity

garners the owner's devotion,
putting a tax on love, purring

theologian of despair.

Figurine

In Degas: *The Dancer, Dressed,*
the straight neck holds a leek-green ribbon,
chin stuck out, half opened mouth,
a sickly, grey face, drawn, old prematurely,
her legs, nervous and twisted, exercised,
topped by a muslin skirt like a tent;
her hair is real horse hair. Ready to leap
from the pedestal, her painted flesh throbs
furrowed by moving muscles. *She occupies*
a niche in the history of the cruel arts,
said J.K. Huysmans.

In the Manner of Animals

Hsin-I photographs by Sally Larsen

Animal emulation forms the basis for Hsin-I, a traditional martial art form demonstrated by Chinese Kung Fu Master Xu Guo Ming in Golden Gate Park, San Francisco. The calligraphy titles by Master Zhang Zheng, which accompany these multiple exposures, were commissioned by Sally Larsen on a subsequent trip to Shanghai in 1987.

熊有戰鬥之勇

Bear outside its cave

鷄有好鬥之情

Chicken doesn't fall down

Dragon hides its tail

鷹有捉拿之勢

Eagle snatches prey

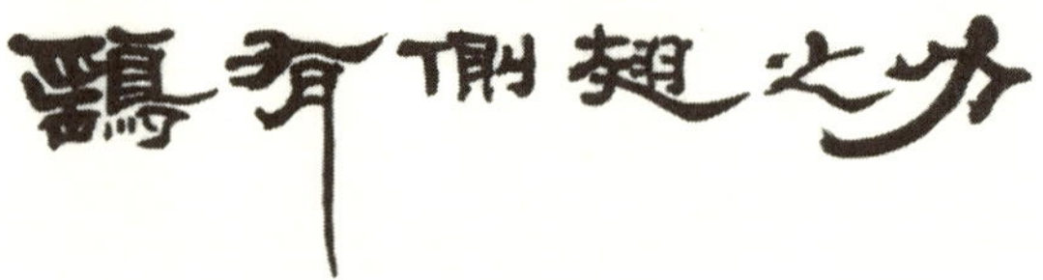

Hawk glides through forest

馬有奔騰之勢

Horse gallops toward water

猴有縱身之靈

Monkey springs lightly

蛇有撥草之能

Snake parts the grass

燕有取水之巧

Swallow swoops for water

虎有撲食之猛

Tiger pounces

Calligraphy Master Zhang Zheng
1987

Hsin-I Master Yu Hua Long, Shanghai
leopard cat preys on rat

Master Yu Hua Long with broad knife
Calligraphy on wall by Chairman Mao

Master Yu Hua Long and Sally Larsen sparring in Shanghai, China

Leonine

he uses toothpicks, the rusty
one eyed master surveyor

whose footfalls on being
never notice the possibility

which his big mouth dining
on essence declaims in roars

like waterfalls. He likes
thick steaks on the hoof,

and compact reasonings;
his preferences are apparent.

Bits and pieces of existence
cling to his claws, essay

a poetry of living being
on tawny grass, on dark

savanna, under a brilliant
massy sunlight as thick

as nails, as solid as a meal,
as heavy as useless lumber.

Lupine

There are plenty of things
to note, existence a plenitude,

ravenous, where you step
and do not step into the same

river twice, the fiery river,
whose banks are abundant

with wolves disappearing
out of existence into non

being. Twigs graze his hide;
flaming branches light his way

who hunts in packs
the smaller souls

on level ground, or hill
and dale, covered with

grass or inviting tracks,
full of party-colored soil.

I think I shall always still
follow the spoor as far as

white snow can to see
to where the flowing

fiery stream is quenched,
taken aback by stiff cold.

Passerine

perching and feeding we lay
waste our powers, blithe

spirits, eating insects,
birds of tuneful song. Lyre

birds, Darwin's finches,
familiar hoppers and warblers

pull steady on the caterpillar.
Song is an image of the soul;

birds are metaphors of spirit:
The Lark Ascending is music

offering beauty to my heart.
Wings that beat the empyrean

mark a faint blue susurration
on the tips of clouds. I had

thought beauty was only pure:
but it is mostly useful, since,

without it, we would be overrun
with the creepy, crawly things,

segmented, that have no voice.

Peregrine

Swifter than foaming rivers,
as wide ranging as forest

and field these merlin,
kestrels, sakers, gyrfalcons,

adventurous in their narrative,
duck-hawk, falcon: royal pet,

he does not defend himself
from kites who lie in wait.

He eats only his food; easily
trained, he abides the falconer's

arm, hooded, starved, disturbed
in youth, weakened in leather.

The falconer is a high
officer of state, the high

falconer of France. Louis
saw the food on the table.

The bird saw it from the sky:
the fast descent, the sharp,

notched, tooth like mandible,
the claws reaching, the whirr

of powerful wings, extended
like the soul of Descartes,

metaphysical and aristocratic
in a vortex of extended,

pliable air where doubt
is banished in efficacy.

Piscine

the psychologist proclaims them
well adapted swimming in a happy

medium which yields unopposed
to their motion; to the genealogist

our ancestors are full of genes
and other good things edible

and heritable. Youngsters rush
for the old swimming hole grown

as wide as an ocean clutching
large caliber encyclopedias.

Fishermen ply their trade
in fog and rough weather;

their oilskins are awash
with spray and salty deliverance.

The Age of the Fish is past
they say dreaming on Aquarius.

Porcine

Much larger than an earwig,
grazing on earth nuts and truffles,

the politician makes merry,
assiduous reader of Aristotle.

Shrewd, smart, savvy, scavenger
hogs clean up after the carnage

of war, efficient eaters. Battlefields
are littered with bloody arms and legs

as they plead for amputation. Drink,
sirs, to my health, an election toast,

cowslip wine; relax with port, as tawny
as the lion you would fain be. History

is your chosen trough: you who examine
textures with rounded snout.

Porcupine

do not affright the fretful porpentine,
his dyed quills which herbal dyes turn
into moccasins for the adroit footfall
that does not bend twigs: witty foxes
eat the sharp barbed ones, snapping
at soft stomachs which patience exposes:
mixed with red horsehair and metallic
bits auctioneers love beaded artifacts.

they call him the spine hog who eats axe
handles, harnesses and the tops of kitchen
tables for the salt, smacking its lips
like a pig and drinking like a horse. Dogs
do not like him; few do and he lives a long
life to get stiff joints, arthritic geezer
who feeds on bark and mesquite who climbs

high into trees associated thence with the Sun
Whose quills are the sun's rays, Whose pelt
is creative energy. Whoso works in the guild
of the quills is secret bound to the company
of women: fringes, signs of power, guard boxes
of quilled smoked buckskin embroidery hiding:

the sacred tobacco pipe,
smoke curling heavenward....

Saccharine

Yes, there are some clean shirts in the room.
Those who drink absinthe discuss philosophy
where Aristotle wore a stomach pad filled
with hot oil. What a great man possesses
is, in the end, only his eccentricities.
the alcoholic fever ceases, the harsh voice
is stilled, the head falls on the table.
To me is the twilight, and the fire-place.
It is well to remember the heroic candor
of youth, as the Polish Jewess pounded out
the melodramatic music from the insistent
piano, the lady whose passion was corpses
and snow. I hear she married an archaeologist
or was it a maker of wooden toothpicks?

Serpentine

sneaky, slithery, slippery,
a barrage of adjectives,
a thesaurus of denunciation,
besides allusions to biblical
texts best left unheeded:
it crawls on its belly;
remarkable jaws unhinge
to swallow prey whole.
The tropics have many
and London has one, too:
you imagine it sliding
through lush English grass,
or looping its thickness
on green garden branches
waiting for plump ewes
that toddle the greensward
as the piping boy's choir
descants in the cathedral
to please a mitred bishop.
In fact the Serpentine
is a little angled pond;
there are no snakes there
above a knight's garters.

Soricine

shrewish, insectivorous: the shrew-mouse,
vigorously insectivorous, unendingly energetic
like (think of a worthy metaphor for one so small),
as History turns its victims into Myth, the sharp claws
tunnel below ground, the blind velocity of moles
murmuring of chitin delicacies, declaims a poetry
of ravenous stutters, savage, sharp toothed,
always ready to bite the many footed wriggling creatures
turning this way and that. The prey of owls, storks
and vipers; they have enemies; unsociable,
they live alone, join only to mate. Some swim very well.
Swiftly, let us sum up their contribution to metonymy:
History, blind as Justice, makes molehills mountains;
History, smallest of mammals, yet gives milk.

Strigine

Let me howl for the noiseless
flyer, the hooter of mice.

He swoops over narrow dusty ruts,
mud countryside, fields of bean

to where weeds flourish in a yard
around rusted garden tables

and a rabbit pen, gaunt pines
and elms gone wild in decay,

the string of dead hares
flayed blue and black-red.

Where the general died
Chinese lanterns hung

over the dock, peonies
in wooden buckets, a trail

of moons straight to the sky,
the skiff lay at anchor.

Last year's grass stood up
dead and tall through snow

untouched under pines, ferrous
stains reaching down gutters.

All life is a preparation
for death; death is a passage

natural as birth. Milky eyes
stare forward: the worst

one can do is struggle
to avoid death.

Taurine

So the King took counsel, and made two calves of gold. And he said to the people, "You have gone up to Jerusalem long enough. Behold your gods, O Israel, who brought you up out of the land of Egypt." — I Kings 12:28

In the TAUROMACHIA of Goya (Spanish
Painter, 1746 - 1828), lost in black and white
hachures, the audience, invisible, gazes
on the god Dionysus, dying and reborn,
as the matador arches his poised foot
and whirls his goading cape, fearless,
careful, silhouetted, *full of adverbs*: obedient,
perhaps, to Carthage, turns, or to the Cretan
Zeus, which bull is nowise immortal.
Aye, from the Labyrinth to the bullring
what thread of History guides the
daughter (of she, named for Europe
who had coupled with the Divine Zeus)
whelping the Minotaur to feed or tear
the twice seven sacrificial virgins of Athens
until the guided swain, the first bull-slayer,
Theseus, snapped the thread of terror
to grasp the thread of love.

Ursine

Bearish, stolid, like he knows
something he won't tell you

getting it from the horse's
mouth in the cave of Plato

where he spent a cozy winter
contemplating the Idea

while you dwelt in error
on berries and ice floes.

With his claws he shreds paper
which tears easily, the grip

of truth confounding black
and white, putting the hug

of rectitude on your lithe
body. He crinkles beady eyes

searching for a fish dinner
or peering at honey combs

whose invisible bees sting
eternity.

Vulpine

A scowl from the monk's cowl,
a tricky smile, a rapid gait,

he trots off from pew to dewy
sward, holding beads of sweat

in ropes like pearls of wisdom.
He excels in historical matters,

quirky, as hounds chase him
through the chevy in chervil

seeking to escape the Devil.
He has a career. The run

of the place is his. He
rose to prominence selling

smoker's requisites and ball
bearings to casuists who ate

apothecary biscuits sitting
on stools which are painted

red or grey. They call
the fall equinox autumnal

in his honor, with good
reason, who divides

one thing from another
with even, subtle, rapid

strides.

&
a
few
others

The Burning of Moscow

Old paintings are seen best in dim light.
We looked out of the window to where the swarms
of the small birds mobbing a crow looked to be
a bar of music moving through the air. One fire

burned slowly like a biscuit of fuses; another
erupted like a torch. It was the peat. The ground
caught fire: below the surface, the seams of peat
burned in tunnels of fire. Mushrooms stood still

as rabbits; they waited for the hunter to pass. Stronger
than an image, it was an apparition: as the burned
and hollowed earth gave up its exploding methane
pockets of gas like bombs raining cinders and blazing

dust. The men coughed blood, took refuge in brackish
water. The twist of a leaf, the discolored bark of a tree
freshets in windflowers, accommodated the industry
of beetles. The eye took in a palisade of burning trees.

Here, inside, the dripping wet of old masonry,
the solid pews splintering to the touch, pigeons
dropping, old icons of gilt and framer's wood,
a prosody of "beaten gold and gold enamelling."

The Regatta

the wind drifted, the spume, the thews of sailors,
rigging, the yawl, the brig, the masted ships,
swaying and riding and sailing horizonwards,
a catalogue of the waters, a Tennyson cascade:
point the turrets shorewards, level sights
at cities: for we have not done with any of it:
the careful diction, a carronade of speech.
Words are like little boats bobbing up and down
like Emily Dickinson. They detonate emotions
of sound and syllable. Not much has changed
for this writing up of the Voyage. We venture
beyond the white cliffs perhaps to Hudson shores
or sunny Italy. Everyman has his own battleship
of nose and throat and sighted crow's nest,
puts up his punctilio of ruffles and flourishes,
fluttering flags and opinions of black powder.
Assonance and metaphor are a kind of fuel. Wet
toes are a figure of speech. I, landlubber,
tried to tell you where I was going, before I
ran out of bare earth and railroad tracks. I
felt a fluid current flowing outward bound
was the best racer across the narrow channel...!

Constable (b. 1776)

He liked the little canals, the barges
and horses, the river, sedges and reeds,
small figures doing tasks, trees bending
over them, the skies above, promising
more water. "I like," he said, "the sound
of water escaping from mill-dams, willows,
old rotten planks, slimy posts...." So
many are the shades of green in Nature!
"Every tree is full of blossom...." Where
he turned his eye or put his step he saw
the truth, as he said it, sublime, *I am
the resurrection and the life*. Living,
he put light and moisture on his canvas.
Soon, skies became the protagonist. "Sky
is the source of light...." An archdeacon
was his sole patron. He was not popular.

Géricault: The Flying Gallop

Horses: ithyphallic horses, covering
mares, copulating: and the English,
they loved horses better than women,
and he knew how their legs really moved;
and he made love to his aunt, a pregnant
inspiration; yet he followed the gallop
convention, to suit the public. Death
was fascination, the bagged at hanging;
the insane he depicted as they were, mad
women in confinement, hypochondriacal,
neurotic, suicidal. He loved to draw
monomaniacs. Male blacks seemed to be
stallions: from Haiti, his friend,
Louis, a passionate friend, a soldier,
he put on the Medusa's raft, three
blacks: Delacroix was the dominant
white sailor at the apex of a pyramid.
He interviewed the survivors and some
were models. He hated the slave trade.
Watercolors, lithographs, of the horses,
hunters, racers, chargers, the great
shire-horse drays. His political
passion received the support of the state.
He died of tuberculosis of the spine.

Or, the Line Dancety

I grasp a firmer resolve,
swept with emotion that I would
sweep you up in it

without any waiting for
stanza or metaphor or
poetry that dies.

You know how they
all do and talk, common folk
and aristocratic alike

at the same moment of time
and in the same breath
of life or poised spirit

as the flame of a spirit
lamp that the breeze flutters,
putting out smoke.

I enjoy the lyric
and I hope you do too
as nightfall approaches.

The Loves of a Cricket (Courbet)

arcane clouds blazoned language
mysterious as the sphinx
indecipherable as the obelisk

your hands bear the marks
of the barricades; wine stains
adorn your frayed shirt.

you are the fanatic, aesthete,
disillusioned by the follies
that formed your education.

You carry a pipe; you sit
at the cafe; you sleep, enter
a refuge from society....

everywhere emptiness reigns
in society: to paint really
is to overturn all modes, to be

individual, democratic, to hold
the pipe firmly in one's mouth,
nose flaring, discovering

the market, publicity, self
promotion, enlivened by

the lithograph, the woodcut,

the photographs of Nadar.
At the graveyard the sordid
burial marked faces with claws,

the eyes dim, wrinkled foreheads,
stupefied mouths. Ridiculous,
this ugly, imperious beauty...!

CW birthday poem [July 15, 1994]

A piece of rotten wood, a stone, the cold
ashes of a dead fire: shine like reflections

in mirrors which discuss the ends of days
resembling the sun shining without intending

to shine: walking or standing still,
lying down, or there is nothing whatever,

as the sun become, as a vine, full of leaves
and branches, watered by rivers which flow

from mountains, cold rain falling over wet stones.

A Buddhist Prayer

I am asking to be delivered from the condition
of famished demons: by means of incense
or prayer or eating food from a little bowl.
Song and music are forbidden me: so I write
poetry accompanied by gestures and the scent
of flowers. With a blow of his staff he smashes
the terra cotta bowl. For the deliverance
of the drowned, they send fleets of paper boats
made of lotus flowers upon the rivers
each bearing a lighted candle. Silence yields
to a pantomime. Almsgiving to the Community...
the Gift... the Way. I do not know who I am.
Perhaps some words are the signs of the Me that is
not the thing that is said flashing like lights
in a sky that clouds up in mists and rumbles
with thunder. I am a waterfall that tumbles
over itself. I take refuge in the Buddha. I take
refuge in the Law...in the Community.
So, it is only part of a beginning. Put your foot
down on a path that leads nowhere, finding
footfalls on stones that shimmer with dew
over glistening quicksand where water runs,
streams flow, to an Ocean emptied of its water.

Yes, I write poetry. Perhaps, it is an act
of contrition. Maybe it is an act seeking merit,
redounding. Perhaps, then, of nothing at all,
in particular of nothing more or nothing less
than nothing in particular at all...winding
around itself to the nowhere beyond... where
empty words empty themselves into an empty
Ocean....

To Erato, e.g., Edgar Poe

Erratic ruses and affronts, shivers
of quips, quirks and curt oracularities,
mixing amber coffee, broad jumping
and civilities, not signs but gestures
quandaries in the present, entwinements
in the past: he approximated elegance
by growing thus, agitated, nervous
beyond the usual. The "man of sorrows"
sang the psalms, rushed out of the church,
too excited to stay for Xmas service. By
New Year, jittery, abstemious, he wrote,
Ulalume, an overcoat across his shoulders,
a cosmic Thanatos in the Bronx in cold
January. In *Eureka*, he found an infinitude
of gods. The universe is the never dying
self, identical and coextensive with God.
"Arrant fudge," they said. He resumed
drinking. He was insane and unmanageable.
A second marriage failed in a cloud of ether
upon a sofa in Providence, Rhode Island,
the empty, unpublished banns expiring void.
He knew "the marble stillness of despair."
He died delirious.

One Poem Today

comes now the metaphysician
mixing up regrets with aigrettes
and the liquid sifting of labial
delivery. can not the Germans
speak but in gutturals and umlauts
or the English but in careful commas?
assonance, I say, is the poet's part,
the mouth doubled over in consonants:
but the unfolding of truth, the revealing
of the innocent word in the clearing
amidst the confusion of utterance,
where the horse enters out of the sky
clattering over the gold tiled rainbow,
belongs to the order of philosophic wisdom.
I endeavored not to use an old metaphor
to express this: that Truth is not a part
of speech: it is an interruption of speech
an emerging, maybe a descending, maybe
a vanishing.

In the old book, the Name is not
to be spoken at all: too sacred
for mere words. So words convey

nothing at all: a covey of rabbits,
their tails fluttering in the breeze,
like animal similes in useless poems.
These are not the same thing: that words
hide sanctity, that words convey sanctity.
That words are meaningless and beautiful....

Perhaps, the spiritual man is content
if he sees
the undulations of swallows on a summer
afternoon....

War and Peace

She opened her reticule
and said, in French, said
Tolstoy, "I have brought
my work." "Oh, don't talk
of Austria to me; Russia alone
must save Europe...." "What of
Napoleon?" She smiled showing
her pretty teeth and unbalanced
lips. The Empress was in good
health, thank God. She wore a grey
dress with a ribbon about the bosom.
The men wore buckled shoes. How
do you get into the mind of persons,
you, if also, you do not have the mind
of God disposed? And the child whose toes
stuck in the crevices of the bricks,
the physical description avails naught
of science. How prosy is war! Nay,
it is the supreme poetry, full of spirit.
"Simplicity, goodness, truth," these are
the divine attributes and goals of our
living: these make our art, said Tolstoy....

Homeric

The wind shakes the trees.
The smokes rises into the sky.
A polished surface reflects
the light. Anger blinds the mind.

Snow

flowers of ice hide the blue sky.
a silver dust buries green fields.
over one mountaintop, the sun comes
to greet the bone piercing cold.

Heracltus Jumps the Gun

the bow and the lyre,
or the word of the poets
writing it: that is,
writing it as is where is
the wherewithal of, that is
as it is: so there: and another
words: the symbols of spoken
words: (are) the symbol of states
of the soul: being images
of things. Things? My God!
"Things die into things"
(Rilke) (Who?). Let Aristotle
rehabilitate the crippled word.
Let us grab the chain between
the spaces. Trace out an emblem.
According to Plato they invented
writing as a search for a cure
for forgetfulness, a pharmacy,
both the poison and the remedy.
It's a gift from the blue,
riding a blue horse, mounted
on stiletto spurs, neighing,
whinnying, kicking over the traces,

the invisible hooves clattering
on the invisible air, “stung
by invisible bees...” (sd. Rilke
who wrote a lot and who was also
secretary to the sculptor Rodin)
From somewhere on the other side
of the clouds I will send you
a post card which you will never
get (receive) since I won’t
survive the trip and *you won’t*
either / or both surveillance...
(emphasis supplied;
imagery omitted)....

The Raptor's Capture

What? The little frog with the big red eye?
From the peep show to the surgical theater
is a hop, skip and a jump: using alliteration
as a metaphor for survival of the fittest. Is
logic dead, as God is? Let us look closely
at the little puddle full of ducks and drakes
and the white swan that swims so majestically
in the middle. Look at its plumage as it beats
its wings in the sunlight. Has it got my poem
written in invisible ink on its white wings? A
French poet is famous for this motif. Logic,
drama, advantage, desire: such are the tropes
of existence. Where is poetry amidst this mishmash
of reality and guesswork? I suggested a scene,
a metaphor, an arena, a debate... a performance?
Hiding in the bushes, take a good look. Pray, ask
the surgeon who gets profit from trauma, damage;
or the lawyer; or the general commanding armies
of water buffalo; or somebody doing something
somewhere in the pages of Wallace Stevens. I
think, because I write: which is as good an excuse
as any. Let us cast our eyes up to heaven
as birds of prey enact the scenario of survival.

Look, stranger, here is the kite, the kestrel,
the hobby, the gyrfalcon, reserved to royalty;
the peregrine, too, who has an abundant name.
You gaze in, your chin resting on the picture
plane, palette knife in hand. Surely you must
be in wonder as the talons are tearing at your
vitals which are in turmoil already at the anxiety
of depiction...!

Alfred Jarry (1873-1907)

assassinate the hallucinating elucidator!
announce the death accomplished
        on a bicycle

precocious imbecility
unregenerate misfit,
the army found he had gallstones.

he lived among owls and chameleons
magnificent gesture...
manifest imposture...
of repeated temperamental oddities....

his act: to write
balanced and precise works
of the mind during sleep

are you able to will the fall
        of the dice?
continue the dream continuum?
choose literary fiction,
eschew biological survival?

he advocated alcohol.
absinthe and ether

(the Lethe of forgetfulness...!),
his artistic goal:
to spend the rest of his days dying
and dreaming...!
to unlive his life, to
become another,..., another
self, u b u..! ...!

Robert Mapplethorpe

as you lie on a mat
your pencil lies on the page (image
of complementarity). In this repose
of objects there is no choice. You

spend your time designing
the horizon. Here is the sea-
shore. Clouds pass in the sky. The sea

heaves. Mishima has written, "To
combine action and art is to combine
the flower which wilts with the flower

that lasts forever." Muscular
are the hands: swift and accurate the gaze,
the classic male. Work is about trust,

an etiquette of knowledge and process
and creed just what the artist professed,
faith and trust and self-knowledge,

like a pilot dressing for combat
(image of spiritual warfare; image of Japanese
spirituality, image of homosexuality, image

of the implements of art). "God gives
us life; He gives us death, too (writes Ms.
Smith)." She mentions the garment she is wearing

billowing in the wind, as she walks beside the sea.
She remembers a friendship of twenty-two years.
"Smile for me as I smile for you...."

"What do we mean by the absolute
solitude of existence? Existence is the perverted
form of nothingness" (writes the grave poet Matsuo

Takahashi). Such is the primary nature
of Joy. Hence, existence is the scandal of Being
(image of the poet as metaphysician). Because re-

production is produced in the production
of the image as a picture (images flourishing
of the esthetics of the argument over esthetics),

the social scandal mirroring
the metaphysical rupture which is artistic
creation, outrageously growing like a tree

(whose roots are nurtured in pure Being:
as here, erect to choose a path,
a conduct wrung on the exacted page);

it follows simply that the lady
walking with her children beside the sea
is smiling as her feet tread the sands

(as, bowing, you, victim, greet your god,
victim of a calling, another horizon...)....

The Children of the Owl

the boy is in the avenue of the birds
the girl grieves in the world that is hers
they are enamored of pools and wells
delicate fountains dying in their basins

her ring is lost in the depth of the waters
(was it by a fountain's edge he found you?)

the scent of roses we have smelled
is as sweet as the tone of oboes

the water, the wind, eddies of light
sparkle like raindrops on the moss

in the Tower,
tiles, grilles, marble
and wrought and
beaten gold-colored
metals:

in the Tower, the Master sees
mists, dead leaves, heath....

she says (but to whom?),
"there was no beginning.
there must be no ending.

there will be a darkness always.

ondine... ochre...."

"oncidium!" he cries sonorously
as she reaches up for the ankle
orchid twirling it in her supple
fingers.

A Temporal Lyric

We are simple folk content to wander
for a short time close to this star.
Time, sirs, is compacted of mortarless
cobblestones. Time, sirs, sighs like wind
through the Pines of Rome. Time, yes,
time is like a pair of lungs coughing
the blood of the centuries like so much
mist of the stars

tortoise shell masks, mother-of-pearl inlays,
monumental drums, megaliths, bark paintings,
what exuberance...! totemic figures,
entrails visible, until the night of mystery and terror,
represented by dolls of masked dancers.
Patterns and colors, the mentally deranged
horror of blankness, of vacancy, of the nothing
that endures

The concept of beauty. Philters of fantasy,
Literature, the "new spirit...."

painting or sculpture? Receptacle: a glass dish
colored fluids, pieces of wood, iron, chemical
reactions. Shake the receptacle. Look
through it.

What is the regime of co-incidence, modest
recording device of the Infinite...? So,
complimentary tickets to a fairy tale.
Appeal to fear, to the attraction of the unknown,
to chance, luxury, fondness, longing...
the drug called IMAGE, to enchanted eyes....

The Path to Nowhere

the strategy is correct: to walk down
the path seeing the enemy horizon
receding. The dust devils whirl
sideways their bits of debris. So,
it seems to be working as I note
the flashes of lightning overhead
emitting rumbles. I am eager at
the edge where one drops off
the edge to nowhere which marks
a slight crease in nothingness
which existence is. I think
of metaphysics every day
while reading the newspaper
which presents the weather map
of pressures and temperatures
and the brilliant conversation
of invented people. Now I will
go to the restaurant; they serve
a dish of courier ten point type
in bowls of fonts. I try to write
poetry at the restaurant
before resuming my journey.
Suddenly, I look up rain-faced:

for, the true poet has come
towards me up the path
a toothy grin plays about his face,
a toothpick of teak in his tight hands,
as he kicks the alliterative balloon.
He invites me to the staircase
by the sea to tread the risers
which flex in rhythm like accordions,
steps, maybe to the stars or, maybe,
to some drop-off to non-Being,
attended by the sound of a silent
gong.

The Zen Teaching of Huang Po

and the trees are very much trees
and the moon is exactly a moon
and the crusts of bread taken with a pinch
of salt are moldy or not moldy
as the case may be as the little
coruscations of glinting sparkling
light (which is a metaphor for enlightenment)

which disturb “the dust on a bowl of roses,”
which fade, doubtless; and the artifice
of the bowl is remembered, maybe, an illusion
of permanence in time, or beauty in mortality, the
classical idea, if I may say so, allied
to Zen meditation. The Buddha, you know,
his face is a Greek sculpture. There we are
conversing with religion, with metaphor,
with history, as I turn the Golden Bowl
with a crack in it, in my bony fingers,
(metaphor for my skeleton, *memento mori*)
who would know (a Presence, an Absence,
a dialectic of Being and non Being) nothing
of it before the knowledge of the nothing
of it were to be known: as my fingers touch
the moonlight, the fingertips of mysticism,
the betrayal of words, the howl of the dog,
the taste of wild boar meat in my mouth:
shifting one’s focus to the middle of Chinese
mountains where the monk discourses, one
paradox flowing after another’s parable
flowing swiftly as flowing waters, pouring
down light silvery moonlight.

The Visit of the Master

in poverty: love of mist and haze
in spring: friendship between us
a dry post on the shore
adds warmth to sunlight

Bart Alberti (b. 1940)

Notorious street screamer, caffeine addict and cafe habitué, Bart Alberti came to San Francisco from New York City. The author of several soon-to-be published novels and poetry collections, he has starred in a video parody of the dramatic classic *Hades a Poppin'*. Now deep into silicon culture and the poetry of software, his latest project is *The Viral Bible*!

Sally Larsen (b. 1954)

When not surfing Ocean Beach, San Franciscan Sally Larsen exhibits her orotone photographs in New York, Chicago, Los Angeles, and Honolulu. She has published numerous limited edition laser books in addition to *Japlish* (Pomegranate Press 1993). Self educated as an artist, her Native American roots incline her toward Asian aesthetics, especially the Chinese martial arts and Japanese screen painting. She is currently working on *The Book of Scars*.